PROPERTY PRESERVATION FOR NOTE OWNERS

What should we do and when

MALCOLM KUEHN

NPL Property Preservation for beginners

NPL Property Preservation for beginners.
Disclaimer.... Legal advice.
Intro... Who we are and our experience?
Outline

1. What is an NPL? Why does it become an NPL?
2. Who are the players?
3. Lender
4. Borrower
5. Servicing company
6. Preservation company
7. Attorney
8. Our place as lenders in this process.
9. The honeymoon is over. Default.
10. What do we do first? Taxes, Insurance, boundaries, and title. (Detached garage? Utility liens?)
11. Back taxes? Tax sale? Tax liens? Redemption.
12. Unpaid utilities. Follow the borrower or the property?
13. Insurance. Vacant prop ins? Condo?

Disclaimer

This has been written for educational purposes only. This is not intended to provide legal or tax advice of any kind.

If the reader needs legal or tax help, the reader should seek legal and accounting help from competent professionals.

About the author

Mick Kuehn started with his wife Janet Kuehn in the Real Estate business in 1999.

In 2007 they opened a Real Estate Brokerage in Charleston SC.

In 2007-2008, the housing market experiences a severe downfall, when the foreclosure rate across the country exploded.

Shortly after opening, due to advice from some professional networks, their company, Southern Breezes Real Estate was positioned to help the nationwide asset management companies tasked with collateral preservation and the sale of REO properties (homes that had been foreclosed upon).

When a property is foreclosed upon and the lender has ended up owning the property, the property is referred to as an "REO".

REO stands for Real Estate Owned. This is a department that lenders have, to handle and dispose of homes where the borrower has defaulted, and the lender has had to foreclose.

Asset management companies are companies who help lenders or banks manage their REO inventory.

Asset management companies hire local Real Estate agents who have specialized knowledge and skills to handle some of the tasks required throughout the disposition process.

These agents are known in the industry as "REO Agents".

Why are REO agents necessary?

Saddled with a very high inventory of Foreclosed homes, asset management companies reach out to REO Real Estate agents to help be their "boots on the ground".

From 2008 until 2018, depending on the area, the REO business was in full swing.

Lenders needed to sell their REO properties for as much money as possible in as short a timeframe as possible.

As these properties were acquired by the lenders, they were and still are, found in different states of repair.

Each property has a waterfall of services that are needed, depending on condition and individual circumstances.

One example being the occupancy status. Homes that are still occupied need different services and procedures than vacant properties.

Another example is a home in the Northern States vs Southern States.

Southern Breezes sold in excess of 1,200 of these REO's in a 10-year period and continues to do so to this day. The advice written here is from experiences over these years.

This book is an overview of preservation and what you as a lender should consider when it becomes necessary to consider taking a property due to foreclosure or surrender.

The intent of this book is to help you streamline your processes to make the preservation of your collateral as simple and painless as possible.

ONE

Intro

What is an NPL?

In order to better understand property preservation, the first thing to talk about is why it becomes necessary.

Throughout this book, we are going to use the terms "Buyer "and "Borrower" interchangeably.

When a buyer purchases a home using a home loan, the buyer signs at least two different documents. One is the Note. The note is an IOU or a promise to pay. The second is a Mortgage or security agreement. The security agreement pledges the home and land it sits on as collateral against the note or loan.

This, simply put, allows the lender to receive ownership of the property in case of default by the borrower.

When this becomes necessary, lender can take the property back in a few different ways.

If the borrower cooperates, the property can be deeded to the lender instead of the lender having to take a lawsuit through the legal system. This is known as "Deed in lieu of foreclosure" or "Deed in Lieu" for short.

A Deed in Lieu is usually a good method for both parties, as it saves the lender both time and money and saves the borrower the uncertainty and stress of foreclosure. One draw-back to this method is the possibility of liens against the property, but that is another conversation for later on.

If the borrower is not cooperative, then the lender can exercise the rights that are spelled out in the "security agreement". The security instrument may be referred to as a Mortgage in many states.

Going forward we will refer to the security instrument as a Mortgage, although a security instrument includes other documents like Trust deeds, Deeds of Trust or Land contracts. Each has its own differences in rights and obligations.

When a borrower is not cooperative, the lender may have to exercise their rights under the security agreement.

This may require the lender to file a lawsuit and take possession of the property via a legal procedure known as "foreclosure".

Once the lender has completed the process, and has legal title to the property, then another set of procedures begins.

TWO

Who's who?

Let's take a moment to define who the players are in the home loan world.

Of course, we have already talked about the Borrower and the lender, but let's talk about the rest of the cast of characters.

In between the borrower and the lender, there is a servicing company.

The servicer is a company hired to receive payments from the borrower, account for the funds, report to the lender, and send statements and notices when needed. They also maintain the escrow accounts that are deposits by the borrower to pay property taxes and homeowner insurance when the bills come due.

Some lenders like the big Banks, service their own loans.

The servicer can also handle other services should the borrower default or the lender sell the loan.

The servicing companies usually use a network of service providers who handle tasks that become necessary from time to time. These tasks include tax status updates, hand delivery of notices, foreclosure, and property preservation.

Property preservation refers to the efforts made by the

lender, when a property is found vacant, to be sure that the collateral property remains in good condition. This helps the lender realize the most money possible when the property is sold.

A Property Preservation company is a company utilized by either the lender or servicer who has people in the local area of the collateral that can perform the tasks needed by the lender.

Selling the property after foreclosure is when the lender receives the money that hopefully replaces the money that the lender loaned the borrower.

Let's start off by looking at what a lender can do to protect the collateral.

From here on, we are going to look at property preservation from the perspective of the lender.

THREE

In the beginning

Now let's take a look at what a lender sees during the entire home loan.

In the beginning, a borrower submits an application to the lender expressing an interest in borrowing funds to purchase a home.

The information provided by the borrower is gathered and reports are ordered that give the lender a better picture of how the borrower has performed in the past and what his/her current situation may be.

This is accomplished through credit reports and confirmation of other things like employment and how much money the borrower has or owes in the accounts that report. The borrower's repayment record can be seen in these reports as well.

Then an evaluation of the property or "collateral" is performed.

The lender gathers all of this information and sends to their underwriters.

Once the underwriter is satisfied, then the loan goes for approval.

After the lender approves the loan, the buyer and seller close the transaction using an attorney or title company.

When the transaction is closed at the Title company or Attorney's office, the funds are sent to the seller, the title to the property is conveyed to the buyer, and the lender receives the Note and Mortgage as previously discussed.

This loan now starts to earn interest and is repaid by the borrower in monthly installments.

After the loan closes, the lender may and often does, sell the loan to another "Investor".

Here is the great news! You don't have to be a Bank to own a loan!!

That's right, loans are bought and sold as personal property. Just like a car or boat!

This means that you could own a loan and have all the rights and responsibilities of the original lender.

This includes the right to preserve and foreclose if necessary.

FOUR

The honeymoon is over

Process overview…

Now that we have identified the parties involved with a home loan, the next thing to look at is the process when a borrower stops paying as agreed.

The servicer should be sending notices and attempt to contact the borrower directly. This is done in an attempt to determine the borrower's intentions and/or needs. During this time, it is possible to work out a deal to help the borrower restart payments and stay in the home.

**Just my two cents worth, but I would rather have the borrower stay in the property and continue to pay, even if that would be a reduced amount for a longer period. **

This may be accomplished by working with the borrower and either modifying the loan payment and/or terms or agreeing to a forbearance.

For the sake of this discussion, let's assume that the borrower has stated that they do not wish to continue paying and you as the lender will need to enforce your security agreement, via foreclosure.

The next efforts should be in due diligence. The status of the property taxes should be determined as sometimes a borrower will stop paying property taxes when they know that they may not be staying. This could be a problem for a lender, as a property can be sold for back taxes by the county and in many instances, wipe out a first lien.

Secondly a title search should be ordered to determine if there are any liens on the property other than the lenders first. Liens could become an issue if the borrower is to sign the property over to the lender in lieu of foreclosure. (Deed in Lieu).

Thirdly, be sure that there is insurance on the property that protects you as the lender. This can be crucial, so do not skip this!

Next, look at the Plat of the property. Make sure that the property is not landlocked. If ingress and egress are through another property, is the right of way recorded? Are there encroachments?

After a lender has found that the borrower has stopped paying, then the account should be observed on at least a weekly basis.

Once you have this information, the first action that you should order is an occupancy check. This is done by contacting either your servicer or a preservation company.

When you order an occupancy check, it is customary for the preservation company or vendor to take time and date stamped photos and provide them to you. Each task completed for you should include these.

Note: This should include occupancy checks, securing, lock changes, winterization, roof tarps, repairs, trash outs and monthly cleanings and weekly checks. Each of these items should be bid or quoted before the work is started. You as the lender should be either authorizing or declining the bids or quotes. Each will have a fee that needs to be paid, so have some money ready to pay these bills.

Once a preservation company confirms that the property is occupied, then they should visit the property on a weekly or bi-weekly basis to make sure that the borrower has not left and turned off the power and utilities.

The reason that this is important is mainly weather related.

If the borrower were to move during below freezing weather and turn off the heat, then it is possible that the water lines could freeze and burst.

Should a water pipe freeze and burst, the property could flood if the water is still on. This can cause a lot of damage. Especially in a property with a basement housing a furnace and/ or breaker box.

Also, in humid areas during the summer, mold growth could become an issue if the power is turned off and the air conditioning is not running. Especially on homes with roof leaks.

Yet another reason to make sure that there is always an insurance policy protecting the lenders collateral.

Should the preservation company show that the property is occupied, then the weekly or bi-weekly (every two weeks) checks should continue throughout the workout/foreclosure process.

Please note that during the foreclosure process, the borrower or tenant has the rights of ownership. Be sure that the preservation company does not trespass if posted or attempt to gain access to the interior of the property if occupied.

This is where we are going to cover the two paths that may be followed from here on. Which path we take depends on the occupancy status and/ or status of the foreclose process.

FIVE

Ok folks

Ok folks. If you have not been taking notes up to now, it might be a good idea to get out that pad of paper and your favorite pen.

In the prior chapter we ended off by saying that we will need to take different paths depending on the occupancy status of the collateral.

We will start off by looking at the tasks that a lender/servicer should assign when the borrower has stopped paying.

The first thing that a lender should do is order a title search, Bankruptcy check, Insurance verification, Tax report and occupancy check.

Again, these tasks will likely be completed by vendors that the servicer has in their network.

The title search is done to search the county records to see if there are any liens against the property. There could be any number of liens including mechanics liens, property tax liens, HOA liens or Federal or State Tax liens.

This title search should at least go back to the point where you have a lenders title insurance policy and /or the last Title search that you have.

If you do not have a prior search, then a full search should be completed to keep you from any unwanted surprises.

Note: If you own the note due to purchasing it from a note seller, a lenders policy may be in the documents that you receive. Lenders Title Policies stay with the loan and transfer with the note from lender to lender automatically.

Liens should be identified and treated very seriously, even though you the lender are in the first position. As stated earlier, a property tax lien can jump ahead of the lenders first lien.

Secondly a Bankruptcy search should be performed. If the borrower has filed any form of Bankruptcy, then it is possible that the lender/servicer will not be allowed to contact the borrower to attempt collection of a debt.

If the borrower is found to have filed Bankruptcy, the lender should immediately consult legal counsel and do as instructed.

Please note, there are states that have given HOA's or Homeowners Associations a "Super Lien" position, where the HOA can foreclose. If you should find an HOA lien, all is not lost. The lender can pay the back HOA dues and stop any legal action to foreclose.

Next, we need to order a tax search or tax certificate. This is a separate search outside of the title report that focusses strictly on the County/ City or municipal property tax status.

Please be sure that this report goes back beyond the date that the property sold last. We are looking for the possibility that the property sold for unpaid taxes in the past.

This should not identify any issues, but it is always best to know everything in the properties past.

However, if a property shows as being sold at a Tax Sale, then you should contact that County and find out when the sale took place and if there is a "redemption period".

If the property was sold at tax sale, some counties have a period of time that the owner or lender of a property may pay the investor that bought the property or Tax certificate at tax sale what they paid plus interest. This is called redeeming the property. Some states have redemption periods, and some do not!

Be sure to know if there is a redemption period in the County that your collateral is located. This is important to know before taxes become an issue.

Lastly, talking about the big three, (Taxes, title, and insurance). We should be making sure that there is an insurance policy that protects the lenders interest in the property, or "collateral".

The borrower should have an insurance policy covering the property from all hazards with the lender listed as a loss payee or additional insured.

This policy should pay the lender in case of a loss and should be proven to exist by the borrower exhibiting a declaration or "Dec" page. This is the front page showing the important information on the policy.

Your servicer should reach out to the borrower if the servicer does not already have evidence of insurance.

Be sure to pay attention to the insured property, effective date and loss payees listed.

There will be times that a borrower does not have insurance on the property. In this case, you the lender can purchase either forced place or vacant property insurance. This is an insurance policy that covers you as the lender for your amount invested. The premium is typically more expensive than home-owners insurance, but well worth it.

If this becomes necessary, reach out to your servicer, and ask if they have a vendor for forced place or vacant property insurance. You as the lender will likely pay the premium. The servicer will then add the amount that you pay to the balance of the loan.

Going forward, the amounts that you pay for this insurance may not accrue interest but will be added to that unpaid balance of the loan.

Next, be sure to check on a survey or boundary check. Try to identify where the Well and septic are. It is common to have shared wells or septic systems in some areas. Especially properties where family members live next door.

While you are looking at the property lines, be sure that there is ingress and egress. This means that the property has access to a main road either directly or through another property via a recorded right of way.

There could be issues if a property is "land-locked" meaning that there is no way to access the property without trespassing. Most states have outlawed selling landlocked properties.

Now to sum up the past chapter, when a lender sees that a borrower has stopped paying, the big three should be immediately researched.

The big three include Taxes, title, and insurance. These are the items that you will need to protect your investment.

Let's take a look at the different procedures when we work with occupied or vacant properties.

SIX

Occupied or vacant?

From here, we have two possibilities. The property can be either vacant or occupied.

Let's discuss occupied homes first.

As long as the buyer or borrower lives in the property, they have all the rights in their "bundle of rights" as the occupant.

This also includes tenants. A tenant has the rights of the homeowner in a Lease hold position, evidenced by a lease signed by the landlord/ owner and tenant.

When a lender starts the foreclosure process, the borrower will be notified using a legal process. This may differ from state to state depending on the state's foreclosure process. Some are Judicial while others may be non-judicial.

For brevity, we will not go into the differences or procedures of foreclosure. These should be researched by an investor prior to purchasing a note or lending on a home.

After the borrower has been notified, a servicer may order another occupancy check, where a Realtor or Preservation crew stops by the home and attempts to make contact with the occupant.

When contact is made, every effort should be made to

determine who is living in the property and if they are the borrowers or tenants.

Regardless of tenant or borrower, the occupant needs to be asked if they are active-duty service members. This is important because there is a law called the Soldiers and Sailors act that restricts evictions when a service member is involved. Please research this, as it may be important to you one day.

The contact information should be gathered along with a copy of a valid lease if possible.

If a valid lease is produced, then in some cases a lender may be required to honor the terms.

The good news is, that there may be an assignment of rents where the rents paid may go to the lender instead of the borrower/landlord.

Please consult an attorney to determine if this is a viable option in your case.

After this information is gathered and relayed back to the servicer, then the lender should be notified.

OK, let's now say that the property is occupied by the borrower. This is where a good REO agent can help in multiple ways.

You as the lender may offer the borrower a more noble way out, by offering to allow the borrower to sign a deed transferring ownership of the property to the lender in place of having to foreclose. This is the Deed in lieu that we talked of earlier.

Whenever possible, this is a good option, as long as there are no liens on the property. If there are other liens on the property and the lender takes a deed in lieu, then the lender takes the property with the liens still intact. This means that when the property is disposed of by the lender, these liens would need to be paid out of the sales proceeds.

If the liens amount to a hefty amount of money, then it may be in a lenders best interest to not accept a deed in lieu and proceed with foreclosure. Foreclosure will generally wipe out most liens with the exception of County Tax liens, and some HOA liens.

So, you see, sometimes a lender has to foreclose in order to protect their financial interest in a property.

Well, since a deed in lieu is not feasible, then the lender needs to foreclose and take ownership.

This can take months and can cost thousands of dollars. On the other hand, some states have a faster and less expensive foreclosure process. Each state has their own processes and procedures, so it may be prudent to become familiar with the process before starting foreclosure or even purchasing the loan.

We suggest that you get competent legal advice before deciding on your best option.

After foreclosure has been completed, there are times when a borrower or tenant may remain in the property, even after the legal action has been completed. At this point it may become necessary to evict the occupant.

Rather than go through the eviction process, many lenders offer cash for keys or relocation assistance. This is offering the occupant an amount of money to help them move.

If the occupant is willing to cooperate, then a written agreement should be drawn up, with the understanding that the check will not be delivered until the property is vacant and left clean and free of debris.

This agreement should also spell out a time limit and amount of money to be paid once the agreed upon terms have been met.

This allows the occupant to move on with some help, and helps the lender avoid a trash out bill.

Once completed, we have the occupant sign a release stating that they have removed everything and that they no longer have any claim to anything on the property.

Many times, we have been hugged and thanked when handing over a check as agreed.

To this point, we have been assuming that the borrower or a tenant is occupying the home.

Let's back up and talk about what we need to do when the property is found vacant.

I hope you have kept your pen and paper handy....

SEVEN

Vacant property Buckle up!

In this chapter, we will cover the flip side of an occupied property, being a vacant one.

Let's rewind to the point that we have an occupancy check done. Again, a competent Realtor or Real Estate Agent can be very helpful.

When a property is determined to be vacant, an agent needs to use reason and logic.

Prior to visiting a property, we have always checked the taxes to see if they have been paid recently. This may tell you that someone intends to stay.

The next item we check is the status of the utilities. While the electric company typically won't discuss a customer's account, most of the time they will tell you if the power and / or gas is on.

If off, that may be a good indication that the property is vacant. Keep in mind that some people could have the utilities off for nonpayment and may still be living in the home.

While on the phone with the utility company, we have also asked how long they have been off. This will help us determine if there may be issues reactivating the utilities after we take ownership. Some counties or municipalities may require a safety inspection after the utilities have been off for a period of time. Some may require an inspection after 6 months, some 90 days. Ask the utility company while you have them on the phone.

Another thing to ask is if there are unpaid bills. Again, the utility company may not tell you. If not, ask them if unpaid bills stay with the property or if they follow the person.

This is where you can call the water company and ask the same questions as the electric company. If they are both off, there is a pretty good chance that the borrower asked to have them shut off and likely does not live there anymore.

***Remember: We need to use our common sense and logic.

Facts can be stranger than fiction....

We have seen folks using water and power from a neighboring property or put jumpers in the electric meter box to bypass the meter. Also, attached a garden hose to a neighboring home to supply water.

That being said, we again are at the point where we send out a preservation vendor or REO Agent to visit the property.

As stated in the prior chapter, the borrower still has ownership until foreclosure has been completed.

After determining the status of the utilities, we now send someone to determine the occupancy status. This can be done by knocking on the door, talking with the neighbors, and looking closely at the property.

If the grass has been cut, look at the neighbor's yard. Many times, both yards could be the same height. If so, a neighbor may be tired of looking at an overgrown yard and has been cutting it themselves.

At this point, compare the back yard to the front. Is the back overgrown?

Is it being maintained?

Is there mail overflowing the mailbox? Newspapers in the driveway?

Next, would be a door knock to see if anyone is there or at least a dog bark. A dog in the home is a step in the right direction. If this happens, you may want to have a visit completed after hours.

This will also help in talking with the neighbors during their evening hours.

Again, use common sense. Do not go after dark. This is a good way to scare someone who has settled in for the evening or even the person knocking on the door, when they are met with a firearm or baseball bat.

If there is no answer and the lights are off, then a calling card can be left.

One other alternative is to post a message in a sealed envelope, marked "personal and confidential". This note should ask the occupant to call your number to talk about possible options or assistance.

.   .   .

OK, so now we have had no luck. No one has answered a door, the neighbors have not seen anyone for a long time and the utilities are off.

Here is where the experienced REO agent can help.

During daylight hours, an experienced agent can walk the front and back yard and see if a door or window has been left unlocked.

Sometimes the property interior can be accessed using a little ingenuity and skill. That's all I will say about that.

During one of our assignments as an agent, we were able to gain access to the interior of a property. As soon as the front door opened, the security alarm tripped!!

Ok folks, how many of you instantly decided to run? Well??

I will tell you that it is not the end of the world if this happens. Simply sit on your tailgate or in your car and wait for the local law enforcement officers.

When our local officer showed up, I showed him some paperwork ordering the occupancy check then simply explained why we were there. I then told the officer that as soon as I peeked in and saw 300 dollars-worth of personal property, I carefully backed out and locked the front door.

This satisfied the officer and he simply moved on with his day with no further paperwork or report.

If your agent is there for the right reason, they should not have any problems.

That being said, there are always law enforcement professionals who may be a bit more thorough in taking your information. The best thing to do is cooperate and tell the truth.

Now, should your contractor gain access to the interior of the home and determine that the home is indeed vacant, then you will want a full inventory of what remains in the home.

The contractor should take date stamped photos of everything in the home and two shots of each room from opposite corners of possible.

While looking at the remaining belongings, care should be taken to identify possible hazards like prescription drugs in cabinets, sharp knives, firearms, holes in floors, slip and trip hazards as well as bare exposed wires and broken glass.

This visit should also be used to determine that the property has the 3 S's.

Safe, Secure and Sanitary.

Photos should include attics, basements, crawlspaces and outbuildings or sheds. Remaining vehicles should be photographed, and serial numbers gathered whenever possible. This includes boats, car motorcycles and any other vehicle.

This inventory should be listed on a sheet with approximate value next to each. The value should reflect what someone would pay at a yard sale.

If all the items values add up to more than 300 dollars, then the lender should talk with legal counsel on how to dispose of these items.

An attorney may advise a personal property eviction. This is a legal process where the property is posted, and notice is given that everything will be removed and moved to the street.

Plenty of notice is given, so if anyone is still moving out, they should have plenty of time to move their belongings.

Note!!! If you are in a condo or townhouse community, be sure to check the deed to see if there is a detached garage. A garage may be included with the property. If so, that garage must be treated the same as the house.

If the garage is full, be sure to have it posted as well! The former owner may have rented the garage out, and personal property that belongs to someone else may be there! Ask me how I know!!!

Yup, Experience. It's what you get when you are expecting something else!

Once the property has been determined to be vacant, then the preservation company should be ordered to secure a secondary door by changing the knob and/ or deadbolt.

I must repeat. A secondary door. Do not change all the doorknobs and locks at this point. You would be locking the former occupant out with no way to access their belongings.

Once you have changed one lock, have the preservation crew leave a lockbox and keys on the back door. A simple dial type of lockbox should be fine and is the least expensive. Have a combination in mind that you can have the lockbox coded to. That way, you can have all your contractors and agents access with the same code.

Now, there are other services that you may wish to have done, especially if the property is in a town with an active code enforcement department or in a neighborhood with a strict HOA.

In order to stay out of the crosshairs of the HOA or local code enforcement officers, it may be prudent to have the grass cut, and the bushes trimmed.

The grass should be maintained at least every other week to keep the home looking like it is not empty.

If it is winter, some municipalities require the walkways be shoveled and /or salted.

While we are talking about municipalities, some require vacant property registration. This usually comes with a small fee at the time of registration. This is usually required in cities or towns so they can contact someone if an issue arises.

Please be sure to check with your preservation contractor to see if these services are needed. If it is determined that they are, be sure that you comply. The fines and hassles are generally worse than just doing the work in the first place.

Other services may also include winterization. Many companies complete winterization regardless of what time of year it is. It may be best to have it done when you initially visit a vacant property.

Winterization is done to keep the pipes and drains from freezing in the cold weather. If a property freezes up, the water in the pipes can expand when it freezes and burst the pipes. This can happen anywhere in the house, including inside the walls.

You may not notice when the weather is cold, but you will find out when everything thaws, and the utilities are reactivated. This can cause a lot of damage. Not only to the pipes themselves, but also water damage in and outside of the walls.

This can be a very expensive event.

Winterization is completed by the preservation company by draining all the water from the water lines, water heater, and sometimes the heating system. Compressed air blows water out of the pipes and then puts pressure in the system. If the system holds air pressure, then there are likely no leaks. If it does not hold pressure, then there may be a leak. This should be kept in mind when a potential buyer wishes to activate the utilities to complete pre purchase inspections.

When a buyer activates the water, it is possible to have a leak that does not become evident at first. If this happens, it may not be discovered until someone notices the ceiling dripping, or a big wet spot appears in the sheetrock or floor.

One piece of advice is to require the buyer use a licensed plumber to de-winterize the property for inspections.

That being said, let's circle back to the point where we are winterizing a property.

Once drained, antifreeze is poured into the drain traps to keep water in the drains from freezing. This also has a secondary use. It keeps the drain traps full so that sewer gas cannot come back into the house. Anyone who has visited REO's knows that odor quite well.

During the initial visit, the preservation contactor should also check for active roof leaks. If it is determined that the roof does indeed leak, then a tarp should be installed as a temporary fix. Water intrusion is one of the worst things that can happen to a house.

As well as water damage, this moisture can feed mold and mildew. Once this starts, it could become more and more of an issue as time goes by.

If nothing is done about it, mold and mildew doesn't just go away. It could be expensive to remove and will hit the homes perceived value from a buyers perspective.

If the power is on, then a photo of a lit light fixture should be included. Be sure to see if there is a sump pump in the basement. If so, be sure that the sump pump works, and the power is indeed on. This should keep the moisture levels down in the basement.

Many times, an Asset Manager will have the power turned on by the REO agent. These bills are normally reimbursed on a monthly basis.

Remember, we are preserving the value of your collateral!

Additionally, any broken windows, doors or other access points need to be closed off. Broken windows or doors may need to be boarded up. If this is necessary, check with the preservation contractor to see if "clear boarding" is required. Clear boarding is when a door or window is boarded up with clear plexiglass to make the property easier on the eye and keep the impression of blight to a minimum. It also allows someone to evaluate if a door or window is being used to access the inside of the property.

Other entry points need to be considered as well. Pet doors, firewood doors, cellar doors and dryer vents should be secured and sealed to keep animals and small children from getting in.

Please don't forget to secure a pool if the property has one. This can be a major source of liability. Some lenders will remove an above ground pool during a trash out. Of course, an inground pool can't be simply removed, so securing it with a cover should be completed.

Once a property is secured and initial services are completed, a weekly or bi-weekly visit is recommended. During these visits, time and date stamped photos should be provided with each report. Photos should be taken of each room, appliances, water heater, heating/cooling systems and gas and electrical panel and meters. If the data plates for the water heater and heating and cooling components can be photographed, then this should be done. If there is a theft, then the serial numbers can be provided to law enforcement and / or the insurance company.

This may sound like more than you would require, but believe me... If anything happens that would require an insurance claim, you will be glad that you have these reports.

If the property is in a high crime area, you may want to call your local Police or Sheriff's office and ask for extra patrols.

So, you see, there are best practices to do what you can to preserve the value of your collateral.

If there is something else that your preservation contractor suggests, please be sure to give that all the consideration that you can.

Once we have the initial services completed and we have an inventory of personal belongings left behind by the former occupants, a chat with a foreclosure attorney may be necessary to determine if a personal property eviction will be needed after foreclosure is complete.

A trash out is when the belongings are removed from the property and disposed of at the discretion of the preservation contractor.

Normally this is done when the remaining items are deemed trash or have little to no value.

If not deemed as trash, a personal property eviction may be required. This is a legal process where a lender's legal professional completes an eviction of the personal property remaining in the home. This can take weeks to months to complete depending on the jurisdiction.

When the personal property is evicted, normally the preservation company will be required to move anything of value to the street.

After 48 hours, the remaining items need to be removed and disposed of.

When a trash out is completed, it may be in your best interest to have a sales-clean completed. This is a wipe down of all ledges, baseboards counters and appliances. Refrigerators sinks and stoves should be cleaned inside and out. The cabinets should be emptied and wiped down.

Floors should be swept and mopped, and the windows and mirrors should be cleaned.

Bathrooms should be cleaned including bathtubs and grout. Be sure that the bathroom exhaust fans have been cleaned as well.

Please be sure to check that there are smoke and carbon monoxide detectors as may be required by local codes. These may be required before the utilities are authorized to be activated.

Now that the property has been secured and the initial services have been completed, then we can move forward with the foreclosure process.

While the legal process is in motion, it may be prudent for a lender to order inspections of the major systems of the home. These include heating and cooling, electrical, plumbing, roof, termite, and foundation.

If the property is a higher value home, a lender should know the general condition. This will impact the perceived value of a buyer finds that repairs will be needed. It may be best to have problems identified and repaired before the property is listed for sale but after the property has become an REO.

You don't want to complete repairs only to have the borrower come back and reinstate the loan or even pay it off.

.   .   .

At that point, your repair money invested could be lost.

EIGHT

Notices and code violations

During the entire process, it is important to have regular visits completed.

While these visits go on, special care should be given to any new postings or letters from the local municipality or code enforcement agency.

Code enforcement officers are generally very easy to work with as long as you are demonstrating efforts to do what is asked.

Communication is key. Stay in touch and be honest.

Do not ignore these. Even small issues can become large ones when left to their own devices. Postings can be as simple as a grass cut request all the way up to a notice that the property is being sold for back due taxes.

Many postings state that the document is not to be removed from the property, so have your agent or crew take a clear photo and email it to you right away.

If you live in an area that sees snow and Ice, there may be local ordinances that require that sidewalks be shoveled and/or salted to make sure that they are safe for pedestrians.

Again, your preservation contractor should know if these services are required.

Vacant property registration can be required, so ask your boots on the ground of this may be necessary.

NINE

Chapter

Ok, as a lender there have been a lot of things that you needed to consider.

Property preservation, legal matters, safety issues and expenses to maintain the property throughout the entire process.

As long as everything has been done correctly and the legal eagles have completed their tasks, then you should now have the property titled in your name. Congratulations! You now own an REO!

That being said, how you dispose of a property is entirely up to you.

One of these possibilities is to sell the property via owner financing.

That's right, you as the owner can sell the property and allow the buyer to make payments to you. This is how a negative experience could be a blessing to a new homeowner and you as a lender.

TEN

REO Agents

When it comes to REO agents, there are directories that you can find to see if there is an agent in your area of need.

Any agent who belongs to these elite organization can help with your needed services. This will certainly save you as a lender, a lot of time that might be otherwise wasted explaining what is needed to an inexperienced agent.

These REO agents are also extremely knowledgeable about requirements and codes in their areas. Lean on them and let them handle what they do best.

Keep risk away from you the lender.

This book has been written to help you as a lender be aware of what may be necessary should a loan that you own become non-performing.

If it becomes necessary to exercise your rights and fore-close on an asset, then knowing your steps and in what order they need to be completed, will surely save you money, time, and headaches.

ELEVEN

Finale

As you can see, depending on varying factors, our property preservation procedures can differ due to occupancy, season, property condition or the borrowers cooperation.

Ultimately, we always want to work with a borrower and help facilitate a peaceful, mutually beneficial workout.

If this is found to be not possible, then it may be necessary to exercise your rights as the lender as spelled out on your security instrument and your state laws.

Following this you will find appendices A-E.

These will give you a list of actions that you should consider during each process. Not all properties will require all the services listed.

Each is titled to help determine which should be reviewed based on your situation.

Appendix A. Default by borrower. Borrower wants to pay. Occupied.

.   .   .

Appendix B. Default by borrower. Borrower wants to stop paying. Occupied.

Appendix C. Default by borrower. Borrower wants to stop paying. Vacant.

Appendix D. After Foreclosure Property Vacant.

Appendix E. After foreclosure, Property occupied.

One of the most important reasons for doing this right is to keep yourself out of the news as a heartless lender who kicked a homeowner or tenant out into the cold at Christmas time.

As you can see, there are procedures that can be done prior to gaining ownership and some after.

Be sure to keep the properties true ownership in mind when ordering any services.

Believe me, there are people out there who will be angry and may go to lengths to make you out to be the bad guy.

Remember to treat each person with dignity and compassion, even if you feel that they do not deserve it.

In the long run, time will prove you right and you will be able to sleep well.

Firstly, I hope that all your loans pay well, and you never need this book.

Secondly, if you do need to refer to the pages within, may all your workouts be pleasant and amicable.

Janet and I send our best wishes to you and yours.

Kindest regards, Mick

Property Preservation for Note Owners

Mick and Janet Kuehn
Charleston SC

Appendix A.

Default by borrower. Borrower wants to pay. Occupied.

1. Have the servicer reach out to the borrower to determine intentions.
2. Perform due diligence.
3. Bankruptcy search
4. Title search, taxes, Insurance, boundaries, and liens.
5. Occupancy check and drive by condition report.

C1. Contact the borrower/occupant if not in bankruptcy. Gather occupant info. Soldier/Sailor? **Do Not discuss anything with a tenant.**

C1a. If military, seek professional advice.

1. Borrower wants to stay, seek workout.
2. Reinstatement.
3. Forbearance, Forgiveness, Modification or Trial Modification.

If you have a successful reinstatement, receive payments, and monitor during trial period.

Appendix B.

Default by borrower. Borrower wants to stop paying. Occupied.

1.Have the servicer reach out to the borrower to determine intentions.

2.Perform due diligence.

A. Bankruptcy search

B. Title search, taxes, Insurance, valuation, and liens.

C. Occupancy check and drive by condition report. Begin weekly occupancy drive by checks.

C1. Contact the borrower/occupant if not in bankruptcy. Gather occupant info. Soldier/Sailor? **Do Not discuss anything with a tenant.**

C1a. If military, seek professional advice.

1. Offer workout. Borrower cooperative.

1a. Deed in lieu (if liens are clear).

1b. Cash for keys (Relocation assistance in writing!)

1c. Offer short sale if needed.

Continue weekly drive by occupancy checks.

1. **If the borrower is not cooperative. Begin foreclosure action.**

Appendix C. Default by borrower. Borrower wants to stop paying. Vacant.

1. Have the servicer reach out to the borrower to determine intentions.

2. Perform due diligence.

A. Bankruptcy search, title search, taxes, Insurance, liens, and valuation.

B. Occupancy check and drive by condition report. Begin weekly occupancy drive by checks.

B1. Attempt to contact the borrower/occupant if not in bankruptcy.

1. Offer workout. Borrower cooperative.

1a. Deed in lieu (if liens are clear).
1b. Cash for keys (Relocation assistance in writing!)
1c. Offer short sale if needed.

1. Borrower not cooperative. Begin Foreclosure.

<u>Property determined to be vacant.</u> *Time and date stamped photos should be required.

1. Gain access to determine the 3 S's. Safe, secured, and Sanitary.
2. Check for Roof leaks, or water intrusion.
3. Look for Mold or evidence of animal infestation. Attic and crawlspace.
4. Determine value of personal property, if any.
5. Get bids for trash out, Winterization, Rekey, sales clean, initial, and ongoing grass cuts, and board up and tarp. (Do not change all locks until after foreclosure!)

<u>Appendix C. Cont'd. Default by borrower. Borrower wants to stop paying. Vacant.</u>

1. Secure a <u>secondary</u> door.
2. Begin weekly interior/exterior visits (date stamped photos.)
3. Begin twice monthly grass cuts to avoid code violations.

Appendix D

Appendix D. After Foreclosure Property Vacant.

After these actions are completed, You should have title to the property.

After foreclosure, Check to see that the property is still vacant.

1. If the property has no personal property, order:

A1. Winterization
A2. Trash-out.
A3. Sales clean.
A4. Rekey all doors.
A5. Place an emergency contact sign in the front window.
A6. Continue twice monthly grass cuts.
A7. Depending on your Exit strategy, you may want to order Roof, mechanicals, termite, and mold inspections.

Activate Utilities if a sump pump is required.

Begin your Exit Strategy.

Appendix E

Appendix E. After foreclosure, Property occupied.

After these actions are completed, You should have title to the property.

After foreclosure if the property is still occupied:

1. Attempt to contact the borrower/occupant.
2. Gather occupant info. Soldier/Sailor?

2a. Is the occupant month to month or on a lease?
2a1. If lease, ask for a copy of the lease.
2a2. If month to month offer relocation assistance or lease to the occupant.
2a3. Check on assignment of rents.

1. If tenant is not paying.

3a. Begin eviction process. Continue weekly drive by visits.

1. **After eviction:**

4A1. Winterization.

4A2. Trash-out.

4A3. Sales clean.

A4. Rekey all doors.

A5. Place an emergency contact sign in the front window.

A6. Continue twice monthly grass cuts.

A7. Depending on your Exit strategy, you may want to order Roof, mechanicals, termite, and mold inspections.

Activate Utilities if a sump pump is required.

Begin your Exit Strategy.

www.ingramcontent.com/pod-product-compliance
Lightning Source LLC
Chambersburg PA
CBHW070058100426
42740CB00013B/2869